Gathering Chestnuts

By the Same Author

In English

Bologna Reflections: An Uncommon Guide

Travelers Tales San Francisco: *Dreaming of Muir Woods*

30 Days in Italy: *The Gift*

A Woman's World Again: *Leila's Gesture*

In Italian

Gente di Gaggio, #29: *Con Clara nel castagneto*

La Mùsola, #58: *Come se fossimo in paradiso*

Nuèter, #65: *Le "tigelle" della zia*

Gathering Chestnuts

Encounters Along the Way

Mary Tolaro Noyes

Jump the Fence Press

Contributors

Layout, Design, Maps—Thomas J. Noyes
Cover Design—Thomas J. Noyes
Illustrations—Loren Bondurant
Cover Art—Philip W. Noyes
Bologna Liaison—Laura Bizzari
Italian Translations—Mary Tolaro Noyes
Proofreaders—Pamela Lawrence /Audrey Tomaselli

GATHERING CHESTNUTS: Encounters Along the Way
Copyright (C) 2013 Mary Tolaro Noyes

Grateful acknowledgment is made to Luciano Lanzi and Clara Castelli for permission to use the story . . . *E Poggiolforato fu salvato.*

ISBN 978-0-578-12761-3

Jump the Fence Press
www.jumpthefencepress.com

For Tom

Acknowledgements

Special thanks to my husband Tom Noyes for his assistance and patience. GATHERING CHESTNUTS could not exist without his collaboration. I dedicate GATHERING CHESTNUTS to Luisa Castelli, to her cousin Giulia Castelli, and to Renato Zagatti. They shared their love and Bolognese families with me. In particular, I offer sincere gratitude to Emanuela Casanova, Yoshiomi Takeuchi, Clara Castelli, Luciano Lanzi, Cesare and Bruna Trancolin, and Emanuele and Paola Casanova. Thank you to the collaborating artists, Loren Bondurant and Philip Noyes, whose contributions were essential to my vision. To Donald George and Larry Habeggar, writers, teachers, friends, I offer my gratitude. Special thanks for their support and encouragement to Giorgia Zabbini, Francesca Martinese, and the Comune di Bologna; to Piera Domeniconi and the Provincia di Bologna; to Laura Bizzari and Antonella Orlandi, BOLOGNA CONNECT; to Serena Gordini and ARCA Italian in Bologna Language School; to Peggy Kidney, University of California Education Abroad Program; and to Massimo Antinucci, Bologna-Portland Sister City Association. Mille grazie to many caring friends: Andrea and Bona Accolti, Sarah and Jack Blanshei, Mitch Ferguson, Paolo and Bruna Fornasiero, Anna Maria Grandi, Diana Monti, Romano Nanetti, Anna and Paola Noli, Elisabetta Papini, Jim Parrish, Laura Pergola, Susanna Rosi, Audrey Tomaselli, and Diletta Torlasco. Lastly, thank you to the people of Bologna and the Province, who have inspired me and always welcome me home.

Contents

Preface

This collection, *Gathering Chestnuts: Encounters Along the Way*, is a look back. Each story recalls a gift offered to me: a deeper insight into not only the people of Bologna and the Province, but also into the world and myself. Usually the person did not even realize his or her own generosity. The title derives from one of the stories included in the collection, *In the Castagneto with Clara*, referring to the unconditional generosity of the chestnut tree as it blankets our path with its fruit and sustenance.

Bologna has become home over the years since my first trip in 1994 to study Italian. The people shared their lives and history, and continue to do so. When I arrive after an absence I always feel great joy. The city and day-to-day encounters with Bolognese individuals still inspire me, while old friendships evolve.

All of the stories, except for *Study in Black and White*, take place in Bologna or in the Bolognese hills and Apennine Mountains, often with local friends. Chance meetings while traveling on trains have given me pause to stop and appreciate the beauty of the mountain world and the genuine goodness of people.

Not far from the bustle of the city one can be in the middle of green hills and landscapes of giant mountains looking south toward

Tuscany. One can enjoy walking in the woods, trekking on the mountain trails, cycling the twisting roads, or scaling those same mountains.

This volume gathers the chestnuts—gifts of every kind offered to me—and is meant as a thank you to Bologna. My personal journey began on the little train from Locarno, Switzerland to Domodossola, Italy, with the intention to grow and to move forward with my life. I thank all of the individuals in these stories for their company along the way.

About the Author

Mary Tolaro Noyes was raised in Bellows Falls, Vermont, where her Sicilian grandparents settled in the early twentieth century. She and her husband Tom live in San Francisco, California. Motivated by rediscovering her grandparents' families in Sicily in 1989, she first visited Bologna in 1994 as a student of Italian. After frequent extended stays, Mary has come to regard the Città Rossa as her second home and is still inspired, not only by Bologna, but also by the Provincia.

About the Artists

Loren Bondurant is an illustrator and calligrapher based in San Francisco, California, in the Mission District. He is currently at work on a comic book. He can be contacted at loren.bondurant@gmail.com.

Philip Noyes teaches Art at Burlingame High School, near San Francisco, California. He lived and studied in Italy for six months and did the cover drawings while in Bologna. Philip now specializes in ceramics and has developed a Computer Art course for high school students.

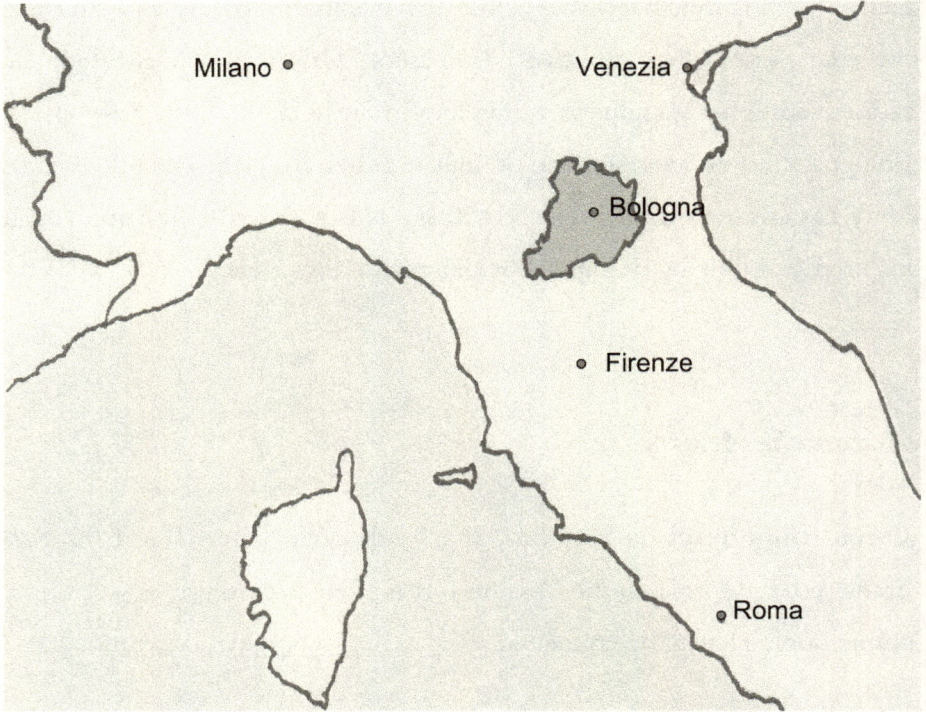

Province of Bologna within Italy

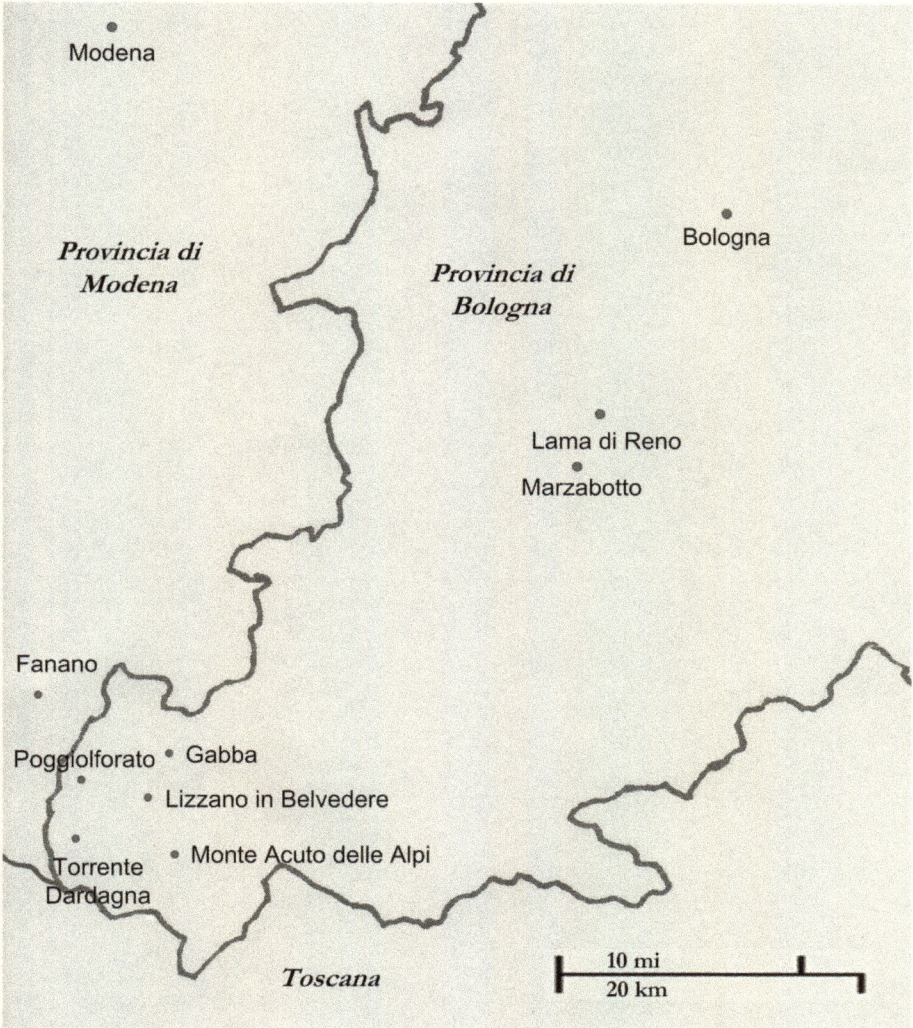

Modena

Provincia di
Modena

Provincia di
Bologna

Bologna

Lama di Reno
Marzabotto

Fanano

Poggiolforato • Gabba
• Lizzano in Belvedere

• Monte Acuto delle Alpi
Torrente
Dardagna

Toscana

| 10 mi |
| 20 km |

Locations in the Stories - Central-Southwest Province of Bologna

Gathering Chestnuts

Gathering Chestnuts

Study in Black and White

Every journey begins with the first step, often the most difficult one. That was the case for me. Our sons were grown and I was free to follow my dream to travel and write about it. However, I was afraid to go off by myself. Life had become very comfortable. Change is difficult. On the little train in the Alps on that particular day, I decided to embrace change and my future.

The world outside seemed simple—everything black and white. Everything. I looked out the window as the train bumped and heaved, laboring up the height of the mountain somewhere between Switzerland and Italy. It was a mid-March morning, close to noon, and the compartment was warm and cozy. A French-speaking elderly couple across the narrow aisle talked quietly to each other and soon took out their lunch basket filled with sandwiches, wine, fruit, and chocolate. Only the three of us were in the small train's car. While they ate, I looked out the window and mused about my life at that moment.

I was on my way from Locarno, Switzerland, to Geneva, after an emotional meeting with family I had never met before. The electric-powered train, a very slow local, would get me to Domodossola in time to catch one for Lausanne. I was nervous. It was the first time I had traveled alone in a foreign country. How slow it was! I could see the snow piling higher and higher on the roof of the car in front of us as we ascended slowly, slowly, up, up. The world outside grew whiter as the snow covered the winter blackness slowly and silently. Inside the hushed coziness of the train's compartment, in the middle of what seemed like nowhere, I began to feel snug and safe in my solitude. I kept thinking, *these are Alps, really the Alps, not the Sierra Nevada,* as my Californian mind adjusted to my being there, in Europe.

The sluggish scenes passing by our window seemed unreal. The black, leafless hardwoods lifted their bare branches heavenward and the snow collected silently and rested wherever it could. Deeper and deeper it grew on the branches as our little train labored to the top of the pass.

The snow looked soft and light, like the kind we used to eat on blizzardy days when we were kids in Vermont and school had been cancelled. It was just that kind of day: an unexpected gift.

The stately evergreens were mantled in white snow-robes. Occasionally an old, deserted stone structure, a house or a small shed, inserted itself into the forest picture. On its dilapidated roof the white snow covered all the timeworn melancholy, except where the holes let it fall through, leaving black silhouettes.

As our train hugged the edge of the mountainside through the pass, far below a river carved the rock. Directly across the immense chasm the neighboring rocky peak jutted up high, its sides flanked with trees, some with arms outreached as in prayer, others standing solemnly—snow-covered, tall, and magnificent. As the train climbed higher and higher the snow outside deepened and everything seemed whiter still, softer, purer, and lovelier. My train window framed a silent, peaceful, untouched world, a gift to the eyes and the spirit. It was easy and comfortable to be a spectator to a magic world outside of myself.

I had become mesmerized. Somewhere near the top of the pass, tears escaped from my eyes again, as they had not so long ago when I left my cousin at the station in Locarno. I felt wonderfully caught—in a postcard, a dream, a film—and I never wanted it to end. What tranquility that black and white world implied . . . and what insulation from the outside that snug train afforded me.

The old gentleman across the aisle must have been suffocating in our cozy snugness, so he opened the window next to him. Suddenly a flash of cold startled me out of my reverie. The blowing whiteness from the open window sent a steely shiver through me; the black and white world was suddenly impossible to distinguish from my position inside. I felt as small as one of those snowflakes at the mercy of the wind wailing through the pass.

Where would I fall? I wondered, at once exhilarated and afraid.

Gathering Chestnuts

Paragon of Purpose

Even one's quiet purpose can bring satisfaction and clarity. I remember feeling buried in darkness inside a small apartment, whose only light came from one skylight, and a window on each of the two floors that overlooked the elderly gentleman's tiny parcel of property. He would work most of each day out there. Perhaps he was originally from the hills or the Apennines to the city's south, still a contadino. Evidently, he found purpose in tending his garden and little courtyard. Watching him off and on over the two months I spent in Bologna, lonely and searching for motivation to write, his diligence inspired me. Yes, I realized, my writing is perhaps important only to me. And so I began to write.

He doesn't realize I watch him from the window. I hear a noise outside and I look down without thinking and he's working again. He is probably in his mid-80s. I try not to observe him, but I cannot help it. This morning he was sawing chunks of old wood, then taking nails out of a fruit crate picked up on the street somewhere. Later he leaned the newly acquired pieces of wood from the dismembered crate against the stack he had already put by, over to the right of his courtyard that is tucked tightly between the neighboring *palazzi*. He normally wears a dark grey beret, with a matching wool scarf wrapped around his neck a couple of times and tied securely under his chin. Now that it has turned chilly, he has added a shabby navy blue jacket, and sometimes frayed work gloves. He laces his high top, brown leather work shoes normally through the holes, then crossed over his ankles and finally tied in a bow. I surmise that he had found the too-long laces discarded by someone less frugal.

I must have too much empty time crosses my mind as I watch him.

Some mornings he wakes me up at seven with his banging out in the courtyard. He never just sits to reflect or admire his work either. He is always busy out there. I think that a woman lives with him. I have never seen her but occasionally hear a conversation between them with her still inside. While he converses, he cuts off pieces of hanging oleander branches, rips them down, then cleans up methodically: the autumn cleanup after the flowers of summer have shriveled and turned brown.

I wonder: *does he invent projects to keep busy?* The courtyard is his world, his purpose.

Is that what we do? We create our purpose in life? He treats his plot of land with care and determination. What would he do without it? Somehow he doesn't strike me as the *piazza* type, endlessly discussing politics and the latest soccer scores with his buddies.

I watch him and I feel a little sad because he seems to have a better handle on life than I do at the moment. I watch him and realize that he has the right idea. He does not wait for someone else to make him happy or assign him a purpose. I like him. I admire him, even though I don't know him. His working in the garden is like my writing. That's it. We do it for ourselves.

Today he generously allowed a young couple to select several pieces from his pile of accumulated boards: his gift. I wonder what he receives in return? An embrace? A friend? Perhaps he expects nothing, only satisfaction from his giving. *Yes, I think that's it.* He smiles and chats with them self-consciously. They wave and turn away carrying the bequest of wood between them, pleased as they leave him there.

And I in turn thank him silently for the gift he has given me.

Gathering Chestnuts

In the Castagneto with Clara

The chestnut forest's bounty and the gift of friendship converged on that autumn day in Gabba, a tiny town in the Apennines. The experience connected my past in Vermont's forests and my father's attempts at roasting chestnuts, to the chestnut roasters' busy stalls in Bologna, and to the history of World War II in those mountains. I had understood from conversations with many Bolognesi that the tradition of chestnuts has a cherished cultural significance. That day with my friend Clara in her family's chestnut forest, I finally understood.

Autumn in Bologna—the *castagne* arrive. The woodsy, rich fragrance of chestnuts roasting in the sidewalk ovens lures me directly to the stand; I simply must buy a paper cone portion. I savor the autumnal ritual of window shopping and people watching under Bologna's porticoes as I peel the brittle brown skin away from the chewy warm fruit and take a bite.

My enjoyment of this chestnut rite evolved into reverence, however, once I experienced walking in the company of my friend Clara in her family's *castagneto*, or chestnut forest, in the Apennines southwest of Bologna. Gabba is a tiny town where she grew up. Occasionally I would spend the weekend there, too. In her wonderfully uninhibited garden in front of the ancient stone house, seasonal wild flowers poked up lustily between the vestiges of random tomato and pepper plants and scraggly weeds. From this garden delight I could see mountains in every direction. Some were green and wooded, others formed by giant rocks jutting up sharply into the sky. The ridges stood one behind the other, marching silently, mysteriously toward the horizon. Tiny towns huddled at the feet of and clung to the sides of the mountains, the Corno alle Scale, Monte Gennaio, and Monte Belevedere.

When I was at Clara's, I found myself looking out over the valley, searching the horizon, straining to see beyond it. However, whenever I am with Clara, the focus is never that distant horizon, but at my elbow. We usually walk side by side, whether in Bologna or Gabba, Clara's arm hanging loosely through mine, while she shares precious moments and reflects on the past.

One Saturday afternoon in October, Clara and I headed for her brother Leopoldo's, down the road a few meters. The bright sun warmed us as we walked and, as usual, we chatted as if we hadn't seen each other for months. We were discussing the evening's dinner with local friends who would gather around her family's table. Leopoldo's big boxy house overlooks a broad valley of the Silla and Reno Rivers. His land stretches far out on both sides, across the road and up the gentle hill. Well-kept barns, cows, and vegetable gardens surrounded us. We greeted Leopoldo as he approached, his eyes squinting out from under the brim of his hat.

"Are there chestnuts today?" Clara asked, motioning toward the family's stand of chestnut trees with the large straw basket she carried.

"Yes, there are," he answered, "but they are smaller this year. The weather has not been so good."

He and Clara chatted in the clipped cadence of their dialect and I stood by trying to glean a familiar word or phrase as their conversation galloped along. Eventually we left him with his chores and walked across the road and up the hill into the *castagneto*.

I had never been in a chestnut forest but Clara had grown up with hers. She has a passion for every growing thing, and her reverent demeanor as we entered the woods alerted me to the importance of the place. Clara takes life *sul serio*. Her eyes reflect this. They seek truth and beauty. I have sometimes seen them smile and, for a moment, seem light and free when she notices a fragile wildflower nudging up through the rocks along the mountain path, or when she engages in conversation with a young child we meet on one of our many excursions. I was not surprised that afternoon in the forest that Clara had a story to share with me.

As we gathered the chestnuts she talked about the past and her memories of those same trees, which stood there majestically, their broad crowns spreading out like umbrellas over us. Clara described her mother Maria Adele and what she had said during the war: "We will not starve because there are the chestnuts." Part of World War II had been fought in those hills. People still talk about the fear and the absolute devastation. The chestnuts had saved Clara's family from starvation. Their fruit could

13

be dried and ground into flour even if the enemy had taken their wheat flour or the fields had become cropless battlefields. The giant chestnut trees had provided them food in autumn for the coming winter. Those who suffered the war still revere them for their unfailing generosity.

As we hunched over the forest floor, picking through the carpet of fallen, saw-tooth edged, palm-shaped leaves and empty husks, suddenly I heard popping sounds, as if huge hard popcorn kernels were exploding somewhere close by. I half expected to see fluffy white puffs erupting and smell the unmistakable aroma of buttered popcorn. Instead, all over the forest in every direction, grayish, fist-sized, spiny husks were jumping off the trees, hitting the ground, popping open and throwing the lovely reddish-brown fruit at us as we bent over our task. The trees were actively generous that day. The music of the popping husks, my friend's quietly murmuring voice, the sunshine and fresh air—I was savoring every moment.

Then Leopoldo arrived to help us. When I commented on the wonderful popping sounds that made me want to rush immediately to the spot where the chestnut might have fallen, to grab it for tonight's festa, he said, "But Signora Mary, if you had been here two hours ago at noon, you would have heard real music, a storm." The heat of the sun makes the husks jump to the ground and pop-pop-pop open. "Allora," he said, "you must return another sunny day in October exactly at noon to hear a real symphony!"

The basket was three-fourths full and heavy. The forest had been good to us. We would be ready for the gathering that night. As we headed down the sloping hill toward Clara's house, carrying the basket between us, we waved goodbye to Leopoldo, who went off in the other direction. Then Clara motioned toward the stand of chestnut trees to our right, which belonged to another family. She shook her head sadly at its condition, the trees so noticeably hemmed in by dense underbrush. "One must take care of the *castagneto*," she said "or else it will die. You have to clean the forest floor; you can't just ignore the trees," she added, "or take them for granted. They can only give to you, feed you, if you take care of them."

Like many other things in life, I thought. *Like friendship, perhaps.*

The Gypsy and the Gentleman

On a train again, I learned how to be kind and to look beyond appearances, even in my own discomfort. The gentleman I met by chance on the train that day showed me how to mature in my travels, to embrace the unfamiliar, and to not prejudge. His smile and kindness to both the gypsy and me were gifts that brought me insight. I think of him still, and the young woman. The experience remains so fresh whenever I travel by train: Is it possible that her beautiful child would now be close to her mother's age when our paths crossed?

I heaved my bag up onto the train at Roma's Termini Station and climbed on board. *I hate traveling on Sunday afternoon,* I thought, as I tried to weave my way through the passengers and their luggage already blocking the narrow aisle that skirted the compartments. I stopped outside my assigned one. I peered in, hesitated slightly but opened the door and entered, taking my reserved window seat opposite the gypsy and her little daughter. I was uneasy and waited to see who would arrive to fill the other three places. I pulled out my book and tried to read, ignoring the mother and daughter. Soon a gentleman arrived, said *buona sera*—good afternoon—to all of us, arranged his bags on the overhead shelf, and sat down next to me. We exchanged smiles and I went back to reading, relieved for his company. A short time later, as the train was just pulling out of the station, a middle age *signora* and a teenaged girl entered together and, after depositing their bags overhead, sat down. The older woman's eyes swept the interior of the compartment as she smiled halfheartedly at no one in particular.

The gentle rocking of the train rumbling between Roma and Firenze, left and right, right and left, lulled each passenger into his or her preferred distraction. Silence settled into our little space. Then the young gypsy woman, in a loud trembling voice called out a question in a language I did not understand, maybe a variant of Italian. We all glanced up. She was looking at me and said it again, staring at my watch, and jabbing with pointed finger at her own wrist. I replied, "Sono le quindici—it's fifteen o'clock," the normal way to answer in Italy. She stared at me, confused, and continued pleading. So I said it again, perplexed myself, but guessing that my Italian-American pronunciation was unfamiliar to her.

Then the man sitting next to me interrupted politely, having noticed our difficulty in communicating. "Sono le tre—it's three o'clock—signorina," he said. Then smiled at me and shrugged.

The young gypsy, perhaps 18 years old, went back to tending her now crying child, while I returned to my book, and the gentleman to shuffling and reading his stack of papers. The Italian *signora* and teenager whispered to each other for a few minutes, stood up, grabbed their bags, and left their reserved seats. Not sure that I wanted to remain in the closed up compartment either, I held tightly to my purse, instead of storing it calmly, as I usually did, and tried to read and not worry. *If the gentleman leaves, I will too,* I thought.

As the train traveled north, my attention began to wander. I couldn't help but notice the gypsy's long blond hair, unkempt, but shining like a mass of fine golden threads. *So, all gypsies are not dark,* I observed, somewhat surprised at the fleeting thought. Her voluminous white blouse hid a slender torso, while an ankle-length poppy red, plum, and royal blue skirt draped over her outstretched legs. Bare feet poked out, resting on the floor in front of both of us. They were tough and calloused, but not dirty, as I would have expected, since she evidently traveled through life shoeless. Her little girl, about eighteen months old, bounced all over her lap, animated, and at times fussy. She resembled her young mother in the golden curls, facial features, and dress. *Madonna and child,* I mused, taken with their affectionate interplay.

Fifteen minutes later, the young woman whined at me again, her eyes avoiding mine when I looked up from my book. I told her the time. Then her gaze shot quickly to the *signore* sitting next to me and she mumbled something. He explained very patiently, in slow, clear Italian that the first stop would be Firenze, the next Bologna, and then Milano. She wanted to go to Milano. He said again that we were about to arrive in Firenze and then it would take three more hours to get to Milano. She had hoped we were almost there. Her eyes filled up with tears and she shivered as if someone had just thrown a basin of cold water at her. *Oh,* I said to myself, *she's scared. Probably more scared than I am—maybe she feels outnumbered here with us.* My insides settled down.

But her little girl wailed just then, so the young woman offered her a breast. The child fed greedily, while the mother sang softly and caressed her brow. As she looked up into her mother's eyes and her little hands reached up to play with her mother's mouth, the sobs gradually relaxed into a smile. They were in their own private world and we, the gentleman and I, did not exist.

After the little girl fell asleep, the mother arranged her on the seat, with a rolled-up pair of purple, crushed-velvet pants under her head as a pillow. She had pulled them out of the almost-empty plastic bag, which was her only luggage. She began to relax visibly, combing her hair and changing seats, like a little girl herself. She clasped a can of orange soda in her right hand like a prize awarded for courage—or a treasure discovered unexpectedly. Then she moved to the corridor outside the compartment.

The gentleman and I discussed Italy and the United States, the world of computers, and the environment. The train arrived in Firenze and she returned to the compartment with a frantic look: he explained, with a voice calm and comforting, that we were in Firenze, that we would be there for a while, arrive next in Bologna, and finally in Milano, in about three hours. She looked at me again, wanting to know the time. I told her and she flopped down in the opposite corner of the compartment. Meanwhile, her child slept soundly.

We continued our conversation, with him helping me when the concept was too abstract for my Italian language skills. He had kind eyes and a quiet manner. A short, slight man, middle-aged, with dark hair and a thin mustache stretching across his upper lip, he visibly brightened when discussing the environment, his avocation. He never mentioned the work he did, just the projects he dreamed about in caring for the earth and Italy's bounty. He worried about erosion and the lack of planning that allowed a mountainside to slide down when it rained and a river to menace the safety of every city and town as it rushed to the sea. The papers he was shuffling pertained to his various projects.

He's a kind man, I was thinking, when he abruptly asked, "Can you guess why I am on this train today?"

"No," I volunteered, "I have no idea, but I can tell you are very excited about it! Does it relate to the environment?"

"No, no," he replied with an even wider smile. "I have just accompanied my 75-year-old mother to Roma, where she will begin her trip to Libya to see the Roman ruins there. I am so proud that she has the courage to do it. I wanted to send her off knowing how much I cared for her and, of course, help carry her suitcase, too!"

Then he described how she had tried to find a friend to share the trip to the archeological site, but each had declined, blaming age or infirmity, and calling her foolish. "I decided to help her with her dream— it's always been her dream to go there," he said, "and now I think she is probably just getting on the plane for her adventure."

"I think you have a very courageous, and fortunate, mother," I responded. "I hope my sons will be like you!"

He smiled, and we talked off and on, occasionally looking out the window as darkness fell in the late winter afternoon. I was thinking about how much I liked traveling on trains. In the small world of the compartment I could learn so much about people, but even more about myself. Our compartment mates, the young mother and child, both slept as the train jostled along. I wondered about their future, and thought *this gypsy is a loving mother, just like my mother Rita, just like the mother of this kind gentleman.*

The hour or so trip between Firenze and Bologna, my destination, went by quickly. I could tell we were approaching the city and began to organize my bags for a quick descent at Bologna Centrale. The train would stop for only a couple of minutes, and I would have a long, obstacle-ridden push to the closest exit. As I did so, the young woman woke up, startled, and blurted out another garbled phrase to our traveling companion, pleading with him for comfort in her manner and tone, just as a little child pleads for warm embraces and reassurance when she faces a crisis.

He explained calmly that no, the train would go to Milano next; we were arriving in Bologna. Then she cried to him, visibly shaken, "San Donato," something about San Donato. He understood. He calmly explained to her that no, the train would not go to San Donato. That was a Metro stop. At Milano Centrale she would be able to change to the Metro and take the yellow line to San Donato. "No," he said, "it won't be difficult. You will have no trouble," he encouraged.

She continued to plead, "San Donato, San Donato," and the tears were right there at the edges of her beautiful blue eyes, seeping over the edges, in fact. She added something else and he answered, "Oh, your family is there, they live there; oh, San Donato is where your family is. You will find your family there . . ."

She nodded her head in agreement, hands fidgeting on her lap.

As I made my way out of the compartment and shook his hand warmly, we wished each other all the best that life could offer. I looked at the young gypsy woman, unsure about what to say to her or do. I settled on a gentle *buona sera* and smiled. She looked at me for an instant, her eyes vacant, and immediately continued her lament to the gentleman, who had been, from the beginning of our journey, a very kind soul, indeed.

Gathering Chestnuts

Cesare's Neighborhood

Chance encounters with Cesare in his San Vitale neighborhood over the years usually guaranteed a memorable adventure. Although nearly 90 years old now, he still goes to work every day at the family's funeral business. We always have a grand time talking about our first escapades together. His latest famous funeral was that of Bologna's own sorely missed singer-song-writer Lucio Dalla.

"Cesare" I exclaimed, when we bumped into each other, jostling umbrellas and sidestepping traffic in the middle of Piazza di Porta Ravegnana, at the foot of the Asinelli and Garisenda Towers. Finding refuge from the rain and traffic under the portico on the corner of via Rizzoli, we continued our conversation for a few hurried minutes. I had just returned to Bologna and autumn seemed to have also made its late October appearance.

"Mary, cara Mary, when did you arrive? Where are you staying? When will you come to see us? How's your husband? Luisa? Your sons? How long will you be here? How was Germany? Do you know we just got back from a marvelous trip to Piemonte, where we ate divine porcini mushrooms and exquisite truffles?"

He fired questions at me *tat, tatta tat, tatta tat*, leaving no time for a response. Fast, that's how he talks and thinks. Although in his 70s back then, Cesare exuded high-spirited energy, his lively blue eyes tuned into

25

the immediate scene. Usually when I ran into him, he was on his way to another breakfast with another friend in another neighborhood bar. Four *colazioni* seemed to be the norm. The proprietor of a funeral home on via San Vitale that has been in the family since 1866, he still works every day, even now. Since we met in 1994, he has introduced me as *parente* (family), although it is only through my friendship with his wife's American cousin that we are "related." I like thinking of myself as Cesare's long-lost American kin though, and listen, amused, when he explains our convoluted relationship to his friends or to whomever will listen. Cesare weaves his way in and out of my memories of the neighborhood of via San Vitale, in the company of saints Ambrose, Vitale and Agricola, Diocletian and the Romans, the Fantuzzi family, Rossini, and the poet Carducci. Often he appears unexpectedly when I'm in the neighborhood, stirs up the ingredients at hand and vanishes, hardly aware of the magic he weaves.

Even our first encounter in the spring of 1994 became an adventure, or perhaps I should say misadventure. We never managed to meet at our appointed location due to my beginner's Italian and his miscalculation. However, eventually we did connect and over the years our shared adventures have continued.

One sunny morning in May 1995 I was hurrying down via Broccaindosso, thinking that I might just stop and say a quick hello to Cesare at his office, around the corner on via San Vitale. He always liked a surprise visit to exchange *due parole*. I had come to know him and the people who work for him during two previous sojourns in Bologna. On the way, I stopped for a minute to read the plaque in the wall at number 20 via Broccaindosso, where the Bolognese poet Giosue Carducci lived from 1861 to 1876 and where his son Dante died at the age of four. The poet later wrote a poem about the little tree he planted in the courtyard garden in his son's memory (*Pianto Antico*, 1871). It was difficult to imagine a garden beyond the *portone* and walls of the rust and yellow stucco houses, with their low, dark porticoes. *Oh well,* I thought, *since the house is private, I probably won't ever manage to see the tree, if it's still there.*

In the meantime, the door to the beauty shop across the street opened and the proprietress Maura and I greeted each other as she swept out her shop. I mentioned that I would surely like to get inside to see Carducci's garden and she suggested that I ask one of the inhabitants to let me in sometime. I was saying goodbye, my head turned in her direction as I waved when—*pumpf*—I bumped into someone in a big hurry. It was Cesare.

"Mary, Mary," he said, "just think of it! Here we are in my neighborhood [he really thinks of it as his dominion] and I bump into Mary! How delightful, cara! What are you doing? I see you have your notebook, are you working?"

I introduced him to Maura and then explained that I was hoping to get inside number 20 across the street to see Carducci's tree. While discussing the possibilities, we noticed that an opportunity had indeed presented itself. An elderly signora with her bag of groceries was opening the *portone*. Cesare took over, scurrying across the street with me in tow. "I've never seen the tree either!" he confided as we made our dash.

"Signora," he began, when we reached her, "I'm Cesare Trancolin from the Franceschelli Funeral Home around the corner on San Vitale, and this is my relative from America who loves Bologna and would like to see the garden with the tree that our poet Carducci planted for his little son Dante. Would you let us enter with you?"

She warmed right up to Cesare. We shook hands and she said "surely, surely, enter," motioning for us to follow her through the big door into the courtyard and garden beyond. Just then, an older gentleman in work overalls came toward us and she whispered, "Ecco, the gardener, you can talk to him about Carducci." She saluted us kindly and went off.

The gardener approached and nodded in greeting, and Cesare engaged him immediately in conversation. Meanwhile, I marveled at the glorious garden in front of me. I had no idea that so much brilliant green, red, pink, purple, and yellow could fit into such a miniature place. And there, on a small mound stood the tree, with vermilion flowers, bright red like the poet Carducci himself described them. It was late May, the perfect time of year to see the tree in its full splendor. *How fortunate I am,* I thought as I walked over to join Cesare and the gardener, who were still conversing excitedly about the past. They had much in common. The gardener's father had tended the garden at the time of Carducci's son's death, while Cesare's uncle had arranged Carducci's own funeral.

Then I asked if I could take some photos. "Surely," he said, "it would be important to have a remembrance of this beautiful place." I snapped one or two of the garden and then Cesare asked him to take a photo of us near the tree and then, of course, decided it would be nice to have one of the official gardener too. So there we were, not only visiting Carducci's garden, but in the company of our own guide and historical chronicler.

We thanked him as we left. He blushed and thanked us in return for wanting to see Dante's tree. I heard Cesare confide to him, as we exited the *portone*, "You know, she's writing a book about Bologna, and just think, we might be in it!" *Magari!*

~

At times I imagine my friend a magician, hovering over events, pulling strings and sprinkling humor and genuine kindness in my direction. One day in mid-December I was trying to leave Bologna, a day when getting anywhere was bound to be difficult because of bad weather over much of Italy and the rash of transportation strikes everywhere. Several heavy bags with computer, books, and Italian shoes—besides the normal clothes and gifts—complicated my moving from one place to another.

"Ciao, Cesare," I began my telephone conversation, exhausted from transportation hassles that had accosted me over the last 24 hours.

"Pronto, Mary, Mary, sei tu? Ciao, cara," he responded. "What's wrong? Where are you? In Sicilia still? Did you get back here to Bologna yet? You're coming to say goodbye today, right? I'm waiting for you!"

"Well," I said, hesitantly, searching for the easiest way to answer all of his questions. "I'm in Bologna, at Clara's. I arrived late last night, Cesare. But the plane left Catania about five hours late because of the bad weather here, the snow and ice and wind."

Paying no attention to my laments about the weather, he cut right to the point, "Allora, you are coming over here now," he said. "You can't leave Bologna without saying goodbye!"

"Well," I began, still hesitating. "I don't think I can. I'm sorry, but it's going to be impossible."

"What do you mean impossible?" he challenged. "Nothing's impossible! Tell me, what's the problem?"

I wasn't going to be able to make it because of the strike. I described my situation. It was about 11:30 in the morning and I was still trying to figure out a way to get to the train station with my luggage for my train to Milano departing at 3:00 that afternoon, with or without me. Outside it was pouring rain, cold, and windy, and my friend's house was outside Bologna's southernmost city gate. The train station was, of course, in the northern reaches of the city, and Cesare was to the east. Normally this would not be a problem. There are buses, taxis, and often the offer of a ride from a friend.

In fact, my friends would have been happy to take me to the station, but a bus strike in Bologna and the resulting heavy vehicular traffic on the boulevards that circle around the city center, had blocked the logical route to the station from where I was planted with all my stuff. Cutting through the center of town was out of the question because the traffic in the Centro Storico is limited. Taxis could enter as well as residents and motorists with permits for work. My friends lived outside the restricted area and risked large fines if they drove me directly across town. I could not get a taxi reservation either. The telephone lines were always busy and, when I did manage to get through, I was told that due to the difficulty of getting anywhere, a reservation could not be made. My options seemed to be walking or changing departure plans.

And to make matters worse, my friend, Giorgio in Milano, had just called to warn me that I had to arrive at his office by 5:30 p.m. because at 6:00 p.m. a strike of that city's buses and subway system would begin. We had to get out of Milano before 6:00 p.m., to face what is normally an hour and a half drive to their home. Timing was an issue. I was going to spend only one day with his family, my last before boarding my flight home to California.

I was worried and tired, but Cesare, of course, was ready to help. "Listen," he said, "wait by the phone and I'll call you right back. What's Clara's number?" I gave it to him. His last admonition was, "Non preoccuparti, cara—don't worry, dear—I have a plan." I waited and hoped, and five minutes later the phone rang with Cesare explaining the arrangements he had made to get me to the train station.

Since his *pompe funebri*, funeral service business, was inside the Centro Storico, the cars and hearses he used to conduct his business all had permits. By chance, one vehicle was available to transport me and my baggage from one side of the city to the other, using the relatively deserted streets of the Centro Storico. "Mary, don't be upset if a hearse arrives, there won't be a body in it, I promise!"

That wasn't a problem for me, since I was not in the least superstitious. I would not be able to see him before my departure, unfortunately, but one of his drivers would arrive at 2:00 p.m. sharp and drive me to the station. I thanked him, my guardian angel, and said goodbye. "I'll see you in the spring, carissimo." My hosts were a bit perplexed and asked "What will the neighbors think when a hearse pulls up to the house?"

At precisely 2:00 p.m. as promised, a huge, solid, black limousine, perhaps a Lincoln Continental, pulled up to the curb. Cesare had managed to free up a regular vehicle and sent a dignified woman chauffeur along with it. I said goodbye to my reassured friends. Then the chauffer and I traveled the nearly empty streets of Bologna's old center in the pouring rain, while everyone else sat immobile in their cars on the *viali*. In the elegant immensity of my own private limousine, I tried to explain to the curious driver exactly how Cesare and I were cousins. By magic, I like to believe!

Auntie's Muffins

A short train ride, tea and muffins, and lessons in cousin-love describe best my excursions to visit Zia Giulia in Lama di Reno. As a child she had lived in Illinois in the same town as her American cousin Luisa. Her family returned to the Apennine town just before World War II, where she spent the rest of her life. Wartime was difficult and she would never describe those times except to share that, because she knew English, she was forced to be an interpreter for the German soldiers entrenched all over the area. She never married, remaining fiercely independent until the last day of her life when she was 93. Zia Giulia's sweet smile and generosity were gifts to all who knew her.

Zia Giulia was not really my aunt, but that's what I called her. Whenever I arrived at the *portone* of the palazzo and rang the bell, she buzzed me in and waited for me on the first landing, the warmth of her smile drawing me up the stairway and into her embrace. The ritual greeting always unfolded in the same manner. She would first ask how I was, and then about my husband and family. Her final question would be the most essential: "And how is my dear cousin Luisa?" She seemed much younger than her 87 years, especially when we would go for a walk up into the hill overlooking Lama di Reno and I would try to match her fast pace.

Whenever I visited she made me *tigelle*, a traditional bread of the mountain areas outside Bologna, with a different name in various localities. They are small flat breads shaped like English muffins, but that is where the similarity ends. Their texture is soft and chewy inside, with a slightly crisp outer crust. Sliced in half and stuffed with any number of fillings is the way one normally eats them.

Zia Giulia always had the table arranged before I arrived on the train from Bologna and disembarked at the Lama di Reno station, just a few steps from her flat. I sat at her table, sliced my still warm *tigella* in half lengthwise, and stuffed it with the delicious fillings she had prepared: a made-to-order fried egg; a thin slice of salami, mortadella, or prosciutto crudo; and cheese, either bumpy wedges of Parmigiano Reggiano or a slice of dense typical Castel San Pietro, or a slather of fresh, wet, Squacquerone or pungent Stracchino. When I had no more room, I would eat one more, perhaps with butter and a smear of thick local honey or fragrant strawberry jam. Then, I washed it all down with a glass of fizzy white wine from a neighboring cantina, or *aranciata* (orange soda), or *tè freddo alla pesca* (peach-flavored iced tea). The follow up was a bowl of seasonal fruit: shiny cherries, plump golden apricots, sweet strawberries, or in autumn, grapes fresh from the vine. We would chat while she worked at the stove and when she finally sat down at the table.

Our conversation always turned to "la Luisa," Zia Giulia's first cousin and my friend in California. Luisa was 99 years old and we had met 14 years earlier in an Italian class. Zia Giulia and Luisa both missed their visits of the past, when making the long journey was still possible. They were both strong, intelligent women, with abundant affection to share with all of us who came into their lives. Their hearts and souls were connected no matter the distance, and I became a symbolic link between them.

I witnessed their relationship when, after I had eaten and Zia hovered over me, urging "at least one more, go on," I would suggest that we call Luisa on my cell phone. At first, she would ask, "What time is it there now? Will she be awake?"

"Sì," I would respond, "yes, it will be a perfect time." Zia Giulia would stand in front of me, my cell phone at her ear, stunned that the voice of her cousin reached even into her little kitchen so far away. I watched her expression as the phone connection clicked open: she would listen, a little smile tickling the edges of her thin lips when she heard Luisa's voice. "Sì, sì, yes," she would say, "I know it is so difficult to continue when you can't see and old age weighs you down." Then she would nod, listening to the excited voice of her cousin, who I imagined trying to recall the Italian words that mostly lay buried in her past. "Just remember to be strong. You know my heart and thoughts are there with you, dear Luisa," she would reassure, concern clouding her face as she sympathized with her beloved cousin's frustrations. I could also imagine my friend Luisa's smiling eyes as she cherished Giulia's every word and tried to put together the Italian phrases to respond and to remember, in her excitement, what it was she meant to ask the next time they spoke.

Meanwhile, Zia Giulia, who moved among all the local family, gathering affection and newsy tidbits as she spread her own sweetness, shared the latest Italian family scuttlebutt with her American cousin. Their conversation would close with their sending unending kisses to one another across continents and seas.

Always disappointed when the visit was over and I should be on my way, Zia Giulia would accompany me, her arm threaded through mine, as we walked slowly to the train stop. "When will you return, signora?" she asked "I look forward to your next visit. Perhaps then we could walk up the hill to the little church at Panico together." I always assured her that I would return and a walk would be lovely, especially after my usual feast of *tigelle*. When the train lumbered in close to the platform, we would embrace one last time, I would climb onboard waving goodbye, completely satisfied. She would always wave too, and I knew, like me, she was already thinking about next time.

Auntie's Muffins

Leila's Gesture

*Another local mountain train, another war, and another lesson in giving inspired this story. I had found myself sad and alone again while working on my first book, **Bologna Reflections: An Uncommon Guide**. For the first time in my life I felt embarrassed to be an American traveling abroad. I had marched against the war in Iraq in San Francisco and followed the news after my arrival in Bologna in late January. I was angry and sad the day the bombing began. Leila helped me appreciate the difference between the policy of a government and the compassion of its people.*

"Buona sera, good afternoon, signorina," I said softly, as I approached a young woman sitting under the shelter near the train tracks. Snuggled up against the damp cold in her ample wool overcoat, she was studying my disheveled look, especially the muddy boots. She looked up at me and I noticed how young she was, how beautiful. Her dark eyes peered out from under a large, dove-gray headscarf, worn in the style of many Muslim women who live in Italy. "Is it here we wait for the train to Bologna?" I asked, nervous about approaching a Muslim on that afternoon, March 20, 2003, the day the United States and her allies began dropping bombs on Iraq. I had scrambled down the steep side of the grassy hill from my friend's old stone farmhouse perched on top, and tramped across a field to the back of the tiny Marzabotto train station on the local Porretta Terme Bologna line. The station offered few amenities at that late hour, certainly not a station agent to answer my question.

"Sì, sì," she answered me with a smile. "I am waiting for the same train."

I thanked her and sat down close by. She wasted no time in beginning the litany of questions. First, she asked where I was from, and I told her, hesitating slightly, "San Francisco, in California. I am American. Where are you from?"

"I am from Morocco," she responded, "but I have lived with my family in Bologna for three years now. My name is Leila." She added, "Did you know there is a splendid island called Leila off the coast of Morocco?"

"No, I didn't know about the island," I answered, "but the name is lovely and it suits you. My name is Mary, Maria. It's a pleasure to meet you."

"Oh, Maria," she said, "I like that name very much. You seem Italian, too. I know many ladies here named Maria."

"Yes, I am also an Italian citizen," I admitted. "My grandmother's name was Maria Calogera. She was from Sicily."

"Oh," she exclaimed, pleased, "so your family's roots, like mine, come from the Mediterranean. We are cousins then!"

She went on to tell me about herself: 20-years-old, only daughter in a family of three children. She liked living in Bologna because life offered more possibilities. She was on the way home from her job at a nearby shoe factory. Her fiancé still lived in Morocco and she wasn't sure she wanted to marry him because he was very old-fashioned and would never consider moving to Bologna. "But my father is a wise man, and I am not too worried that he will insist I marry him," she said. As an afterthought she added, "My brothers are impossible, though. They are like my fiancé." When I asked about her mother Leila had little to say. "She stays home and would prefer that I follow her path, which I don't want to do."

"Well, then," I responded, "tell me about the life you wish for."

"No, first you must tell me about yourself, signora. Perhaps I have been talking too much."

"No, you are not talking too much, Leila," I assured her. "I am a writer and I learn so much when I meet people like you."

The train rumbled slowly into the station and we walked together, climbing on board and into an almost empty car. We sat down opposite each other, next to the window.

I explained my reason for being in Bologna since early autumn, with only a brief trip home for the Christmas holiday, that the editor of my book on Bologna lived there in Marzabotto, and we were collaborating as I revised and updated the material.

She had plenty of questions and relished our chance encounter. I described my family and our lives in California and asked, "Would you like to study at Bologna's famous university, Leila?"

"No," she replied, "studying doesn't interest me. I want to earn money so that I can be independent, too, like your sons. I want a future in Bologna, so perhaps you can tell me about her history."

"Where do you live?" I asked. "I could describe your neighborhood's past."

"We are just inside Porta Lame," she said, "and it doesn't seem very interesting to me!"

Then I described how she would have found it in the Middle Ages and Renaissance. "Just imagine the canal that once flowed where via Riva di Reno is now, and the silk factories humming, turning out cloth, making the Bolognesi rich and famous. Bombs destroyed the neighborhood during World War II." I grew pensive and said, "What you see has been rebuilt since then. We have lost so much."

The perfect opening . . .

Without missing a beat, her large expressive eyes, fringed with thick, black lashes, locked with mine, and I understood where our conversation was headed. My heart leaped up to my throat.

"Signora Maria," she said, her husky voice quiet, yet strong, "do you know what happened this morning?"

I know we must have blinked but when I think back to that moment, it seems like even the miniscule flick of an eyelid would have severed the connection. "Sì, Leila. Yes, I know what happened this morning and I'm so sorry."

As I said it, my hands flew up and covered my eyes and the sobs, which had been caged deep inside me for weeks, exploded into the space between us. For the first time in my life I was ashamed to be an American. I had protested in the streets, signed petitions, and voted, realizing finally that bombs were inevitable, and that the American people were seemingly powerless against our government, which marched the world toward war.

She listened quietly. I could feel her eyes watching me as I sat there that afternoon in March. "I'm so sorry, so ashamed of my country; so sorry, *vergogna*—shame . . ."

In the silence, Leila looked up again, reached across the space between us and took my hands in hers. "Don't worry, Signora Maria," she whispered, "I understand. I understand that we must separate the actions of governments from the individuals that we meet. I can do that. Please don't be so sad. We have to understand each other and talk to each other. I understand." While she spoke, her eyes stayed focused on our joined hands and then she looked up at me watching her.

"Grazie Leila," I said. "Thank you for understanding, and I hope together we can help to change . . ."

And she suddenly asked me, "Signora, do you know that the date of my birth is May 11? When is your birthday?"

Astonished, I answered, "My birthday is also May 11, Leila."

So, we sat together on the little train chugging toward Bologna, our hands still clasped, and my lovely companion met my gaze boldly and announced, without the slightest hesitation, "Our souls were meant to connect today, Signora Maria, don't you think?"

Leila's Gesture

Gathering Chestnuts

Luciano's Story

Even in wartime, the goodness of humankind can triumph. Luciano's accounts of his experiences as a partisan in the Bolognese Apennines during World War II often describe the suffering of the mountain people, the violence and the horror. However, this story, especially important to him, offers hope that in the end, goodwill and peace persist. Thank you for the gift of your story, Luciano.

My friend Luciano was 89 years old when we met in 2010 at Clara's house. Like her, he had grown up in a village near Lizzano in Belevedere, in the Apennines to the southwest of Bologna. He's not much taller than my 5 feet 2 inches; a handsome gentleman with plenty of wavy white hair combed back, lively eyes, and a very friendly smile. My first impression was *Oh my goodness, how young he seems!* In fact, he had just walked from his house on the other side of Bologna. Before that, he had been on the roof of his house in the mountains, repairing it. While Luciano does not just live in the past, the stories of his youth and life during World War II are engaging and revealing. A good storyteller, he shares details about his role as a partisan fighting against the Fascists and the Nazis and the insights gleaned from those moments.

When I asked him how he became part of the partisan movement operating in his home territory, he described first his time as an Italian foot soldier from January 1941, fighting primarily in Slovenia and

49

Croatia, until his release in August 1943. He returned home to Ca' di Julio in the Bolognese Apennines and with his discharge papers from the Italian military, the possibility of a job near there. In the meantime, Mussolini and the Fascists had been overthrown in Italy and the Germans were afraid Italy would join with the Allied forces. They created a Nazi puppet state known as the Italian Social Republic (RSI), or the Republic of Salò (1943-45) as it was commonly called.

When in April 1944 Luciano was ordered to present himself for the mandatory physical exam before being conscripted into the RSI, he chose instead to join the partisans active in the area, on the side fighting against the Fascists and Nazis. His previous wartime military experience and knowledge of the geography of the territory allowed him to play a leadership role in their activities.

The many small bands of partisans were connected mostly by the *staffette*, messengers, who brought orders, munitions, and news back and forth between the groups. The levels of experience of the soldiers varied as did the range of armaments each group had at its disposal. Luciano described the many difficulties they faced, a very significant one being the nature of the conflict as a civil war. Knowing whether a partisan volunteer was actually a spy or if a neighbor was a Fascist supporter kept the tension high among the locals. The entrenched German army in the area, not to mention the territory's challenging geography and the lack of food and supplies, created a perilous situation.

Along with the many stories of unpardonable violence, cruelty, and bloodshed during the war, Luciano relates this one that offers faith in the decency of human kind.

. . . And Poggiolforato Was Saved

By Luciano Lanzi

It was the end of August 1944. My squadron, which was part of the Seventh Garibaldi Brigade, was housed at Ca' di Lanzi, located on the slope of Monte della Riva to the left of the Torrente Dardagna. One morning our commander Armandino ordered the squad to head out and patrol the area around the Masera Pass, where the Germans were securely entrenched. Our group of about 10 well-armed partisans, mostly in our early twenties, departed convinced that we would not encounter any trouble. In about 20 minutes when we arrived on the hill overlooking the Masera Pass, near the provincial road for Fanano, which we called Mulin e'd' Codghin, we observed four German soldiers in a field loading hay from a haystack onto a cart pulled by two horses. We fired on them and the platoon's commander, Armandino, ordered them to surrender. Two dropped their guns and raised their arms immediately and we took them prisoners while the other two tried to flee. We fired. One soldier managed to get away, but the other one caught a bullet in a leg and fell injured to the ground. We loaded the injured soldier on the surviving horse, the other having been killed during the skirmish, and took off for our base camp.

Setting off on the paved Farnè road as far as Plinardo, we then took a path that descended quickly to Ca' di Julio, crossed the bridge over the Dardagna and arrived, without incident, at our base Ca' di Lanzi. The injured soldier had screamed in German during the entire trip, while the other two prisoners followed without resistance. All of them were Austrian and older than us. Our return was quick and uneventful.

The day evolved into a challenging and unsettled one. The injured man continued to cry out in pain and fear. We realized that a doctor was needed, but at first none came to mind. Eventually I remembered one who had tended my injured hand a while ago. That evening under cover of darkness, five or six of us left to get him at Vidiciatico where he lived. We arrived in about a half hour and introduced ourselves, explaining the problem. He asked me where the injured soldier was and I replied that he should just follow us and not ask any questions. He did.

When we got back to the camp, the prisoner-patient raged against us, calling us bandits who were forcing him to undergo the operation and would then surely kill him. In spite of the stressful circumstances and the difficulty of the operation, the doctor performed the surgery competently and left the patient with us.

However, our group included a Polish partisan, an electrical engineer, who had been transferred to Italy from a German prison camp and forced to work with the Italian Fascists. He escaped and joined us. His job in our squad was to handle the radio transmissions with the Allied forces. In Poland the Nazis had exterminated his family and naturally he harbored a ferocious hate. He was insistent on killing the injured soldier and so we had to keep a constant watch on him. Armandino dispatched a runner to the *Comando di Brigata* to explain the situation, since it was impossible for our group to function and at the same time keep the prisoner safe. Within a short time the messenger returned with the order to take the injured soldier and the two other prisoners to the town of Poggiolforato; a doctor who tended to the medical needs of the partisans was there along with others to guard the prisoners. That freed us to patrol the lower area of the Torrente Dardagna, which was our mission.

A few weeks of calm followed.

And then the news arrived from our compatriots, a Tuscan squad of partisans, informing us that the main contingent of the Nazi army was on the march and would soon arrive at the crest of the Apennines. From our position on the twenty-seventh of September we saw the troops closing in, descending from the Spigolino and the Tavola del Cardinale, which we called the Pian della Faggia della Saetta. It was afternoon and we had good cover and visibility through the shrubs and grasses.

At the Vergine (Church of Santa Maria del Faggio), the ranking officer of the German army, armed heavily with mortars, took position. Groups of search parties descended by way of the via dell'Acerone. When they reached the Casetta della Boctia, some partisans, who were posted there as lookouts, fired when they saw the first Germans. A small encounter ensued in which one partisan was killed. Another was injured and another captured. No German soldier either died or was injured during that skirmish.

Unfortunately though, an immediate Nazi reprisal followed: the inhabitants in the area of Ca' di Berna were rounded up and herded into the kitchen of one of the houses, which happened to belong to my brother-in-law Giglio Taglioli. They were all shot.

In the meantime, a dense fog descended and it began to drizzle. After the massacre, the SS reconnaissance group descended onto the main road and the Nazi troops amassed in the town of Poggiolforato. Since the partisans camped there were not prepared to engage in combat, they quickly escaped. The Nazis again rounded up all the inhabitants—women, men, and children—and grouped them in front of the millers Augusto and Aldo's house.

They were preparing to shoot everyone, about 100 people. Suddenly in the midst of the confusion, the German soldier, the one we had injured and subsequently taken care of and protected, appeared and presented himself to the commander. In Poggiolforato he had been guarded and cared for by a partisan, Gianna Castelli, a young woman of about 25 years old. As the situation was evolving in the town, she had let him escape. When he approached his fellow soldiers he recounted the story of his capture, of the care he had received and of the kind treatment and attention of the town's people. He was convincing enough that the Nazi commander suspended the execution and every form of retribution, including the intended burning of the all the houses.

. . . And Poggiolforato was saved.

While this had been going on, my companions and I, about 15 of us, were at Plinardo, posted with two assault rifles, watching the road from Vidiciatico to Querciola. We knew nothing about the encounter and its devastating results at Ca' di Berna. When the news from Poggiolforato reached us, I was deeply touched. The human decency and proper behavior of both the partisans and the local people toward one wounded enemy prisoner, in the midst of the violence and hatred of war, had saved Poggiolforato. —L.L.

Editor's Note:

Records show that from September 8, 1943, to April 25, 1945, especially in the summer of 1944, probably due to the swelling in the ranks of the partisans, hundreds of episodes like that at Ca' di Berna were conducted by the Fascists and the Nazis against the civil population in the territory near the Gothic Line. The partisans were considered terrorists and criminals by the government forces, against which any repressive means were legitimate.

Gathering Chestnuts

Mountain Climbing

Facing any mountain climb with a friend is always recommended. The surrounding beauty, the intense effort, and the rewards at the end of the labor, are unforgettable. Sharing the moment becomes a lovely part of the experience.

C lara and I arrived at the parking lot in Lizzano in Belvedere right on time, excited about our hike that early Sunday morning. The plan was to walk from Lizzano in Belevedere to Monte Acuto delle Alpi, from one valley to the other, one town to the other. I had no idea what that meant; only that we would climb a mountain, and Clara was very pleased to share her mountains with me.

Sergio would be our leader and he came to greet us, wearing his Alpino soldier's hat, asserting his authority immediately. His experience in the Italian military as an alpine soldier in the Alps defined him. He is devoted to his mountains. Clara introduced me, and Sergio immediately extended his right hand in greeting, "Buon giorno, signora, welcome, but those shoes are not adequate for this hike. Are you sure you should join us?"

I looked at Clara, she at me, and then we both answered at once, "Sì!"

"Absolutely yes, I'll be okay," I added quickly, sounding more secure than I felt.

Sergio shook his head and turned to welcome the other trekkers who would join us. Clara and I decided that we would try, and if the hike became too difficult in my sporty, strapped Mary Jane shoes, she could get us back to the trailhead.

When the six of us had gathered—Sergio, Giorgio, Santo, Luciano, Clara, and me—we started our hike into the woods. It was 7:30 a.m. and we planned to arrive at our destination by about 5:30 that afternoon. As we left Lizzano in Belvedere, the sky threatened rain and the morning chill bordered on cold. The pace was fast with Sergio at the lead and we kept up with little trouble, in spite of the challenge of mud, rocks, and tree roots. We marched through woods and fields, up and down hills, across rock formations, up, down, over, slipped, fell, brushed off mud, dirt, not quite keeping up with the pace of our agile leader. Clearly, his goal was reaching the end as quickly as possible. No stopping to smell the flowers along the way for him. Clara and I focused our attention elsewhere though. Our goal was to enjoy the exquisite scenery and breathe the beauty of little things along the way: a yellow or pink wildflower poking up among the rocks or a wave of fog shrouding the neighboring green hill. We managed quite well, although usually tagging a short distance behind. But they never had to wait for us, so Sergio relaxed and our group became a cohesive pack of Sunday excursionists.

Monte Gennaio's colossal stony summit, thrust high up into the sky, punctuated the panoramas that stretched along the gorges, ravines, and gullies far into the mysterious distant greyness. Several shades of green changed according to the light, the mist, or the curve of the land. The lemony green of the fields contrasted with the beech forests, tall trees with distorted trunks, sinewy forms that forever follow the commands of the gusty wind. Dark olive green stubs of weeds lined the trail, but then willowy fragile ones would catch the light and our attention, and even sparkle.

With Clara and her friends that day, I remember narrow, often steep, muddy trails lined with brave early summer mountain wildflowers; mounds of slowly melting snow; the sound and force of the cold wind whistling past in the flat stretches, tunneled by the surrounding hills and mountains; the rounded humpbacked hills and mountains stretching into the horizon, covered completely with green bushes and hardwood trees. The veil of mist made the scene a mystical mountain march.

Then there were the birds, the soaring, dipping, hovering big ones, and the chirping, fluttering, hopping little ones. Tiny insects labored across our path or landed on a promising leaf or petal, oblivious to our presence. Sometimes the tepid warmth of the sun managed to peak through the often dense clouds or a stand of trees to warm our faces and the backs of our necks as we trekked along the path. My companions' voices, mostly Clara's, added to the music all around us as onward we went, often single file to turn the next bend or climb the next rocky outcrop.

I remember the fog that wrapped a desolate mountain in a tender shawl; the ancient tumbling-down houses of grey rocks, hidden, silent, with histories lost to us; the tiny, newly born beech trees under the watchful eye of their elders; the infinite game between darkness and light; and the tiny villages that hugged the side of the mountains.

Clara seemed a beautiful multicolored butterfly flitting among the yellow, white, and violet flowers that covered the edges of the trail. My friend is the happiest when she is in her mountains. I also remember the smiles and chatter of the other companions. Santo brought and shared a real *pranzo*, complete with red wine and sharp cheese and, even a *caffè* from his thermos served in tiny plastic cups. Sergio shared his knowledge of history and of the mountains, and was quite patient with me, the foreign *signora* with the inadequate shoes. We occasionally changed partners as we pressed forward: Santo and I exchanged many stories about Sicily because of our shared Sicilian heritage.

Finally, I remember the wet and cold and the exhaustion at the trail's end as we entered Monte Acuto delle Alpi from above, along the grey stone road. At the trek's end we sat along the roadside's stone wall, grabbing a drink of water, gabbing like school kids, waiting for our rides back home.

"We climbed the mountain, Clara!"

"Sì, sì, my friend," she answered.

What a gift!

The Gift

Life in Bologna on my first visit was magical. I was living in a medieval city, learning Italian, and doing exactly what I wanted to do. I was often lonely, but little by little I learned to explore life in Bologna's streets, practice my Italian, and try to understand the life in and history of an ancient city that was slowly but surely seducing me. I am not a musician, but music has always filled my life with beauty. Bologna's musical legacy is rich, as I discovered one memorable day.

I pushed open the heavy wooden door of a music store called Orpheus and entered into a small room overflowing with university students, racks of sheet music, ancient instruments, and shiny new ones. Guitars, violins, and even an exotic item or two—a drum from Africa and a wooden flute from South America—hung from floor to ceiling, covering every inch of wall space. The large display window had caught my attention as I wandered in the narrow, porticoed streets of Bologna's university district. I would be leaving for home in a couple of days and I still had to buy my son the gift he had requested. Orpheus seemed the perfect place.

A gentleman approached immediately, in spite of the chaos. He was perhaps in his early forties, short, with black hair and thick, dark-rimmed glasses. His large doe-eyes smiled in welcome, as he asked in formal Italian, "Prego, signora, can I assist you?"

"Sì, signore, grazie," I responded. "I'm looking for a gift for my son, who is a musician and requested an alto recorder. I see you have a number of recorders here in the display," and I turned to the glass cabinet to my right. "But I can't distinguish an alto from a soprano!"

"Benissimo," he said, his eyes animated all at once. "It would please me to assist you. You see the alto recorder is my specialty. I teach students from the university and I play in a small professional ensemble." Unlocking the cabinet, he continued, "Please tell me about your son. What is his name?"

"Si chiama Filippo—his name is Philip," I answered, and then described him to the professor, his musical experience and his personality: a young man of 18, talented, whose soul the world glimpsed when he played thin, lilting melodies on his soprano recorder, or on his flutes and pipes from around the world.

He shook his head slowly as he closed the display and earnestly explained, "Signora, these instruments will not satisfy your son's needs. I'm sorry. They are for people without serious intention or perhaps for beginners. Do you have some time you can spend here while I demonstrate my meaning?"

"Yes, of course," I answered, anxious to bring home a wonderful gift for my son. "I would appreciate your assistance, Professore."

So he led me out of the tiny, crowded room; we slithered snake-like through the store's narrow inner passages, deep into the cave-like chambers in the back, through a room dedicated to lutes and stringed instruments that hung on the dark walls, back, back, into another recess full of flutes, recorders, oboes, and clarinets. He motioned me to a comfortable, overstuffed chair. I sat down, already somewhat enchanted, while he instructed his young assistant to run next door to the bar and get us each a caffè.

In the meantime, he selected seven alto recorders made of wood, each a different shade of rich brown. He lined them up on a small, round, mahogany parlor table and described the wood of each instrument, its characteristic sound, and special qualities. As he talked, his hands gently caressed the smooth surface of the recorder he held while his twinkling eyes communicated pleasure.

When the young assistant arrived with our caffè, he thanked her, encouraged her to join us, and proceeded to entertain us with strains of Bach, Vivaldi, and Mozart to demonstrate the particularities of each instrument. Encouraging me to choose the one or two most appropriate for my son's musical style, he exclaimed "Brava, signora," pleased when I tentatively made my selections. "You have a good ear. You have chosen well, and now I will help you make the final selection."

With that, he immediately segued into Renaissance court music, demonstrating not only the instrument's vibrancy but also his own talent and delight in playing. I felt like a guest in his living room, the private concert a gift from a musician's soul. Thoughts of Orpheus and his musical magic flitted through my mind as lovely melodies filled the resonant space.

I admitted after he had finished that I could not distinguish between the two. I said, "Professore, I cannot decide. The beauty of the music confounds me. They are both eloquent. Please help me?"

"You are correct," he responded with deference, "they are both truly fine instruments. I understand your confusion. But I will play them each again, explain the sound, and help you decide. Relax for a moment more, please, signora."

I listened while he played. In the end logic did not help me decide. I chose one over the other only because its rich tones pulled at me more strongly. Its wood was golden and polished smooth. Fine detailed bands were etched around the ends of each tightly fitted section. Subtle hues of the chestnut grain glowed from deep inside. When I held it, I could feel the warmth of the wood. I imagined the instrument in Philip's hands while he, too, would serenade me.

We returned to the front of the store and continued our conversation as I paid for the gift. The professor, animated and content, explained the proper care of the recorder and packaged it for the long trip to California. I assured him as we parted, shaking hands, that yes, I would encourage my son to someday make a pilgrimage to Bologna and the music store Orpheus. Perhaps they could then share a moment of music. I thanked him for his help and he waved as I closed the door behind me.

I exited onto the narrow sidewalk, the darkness creeping slowly into the medieval streets. I hurried on via Marsala toward Piazza Rossini and home, the professor's music still echoing inside my head. As I crossed the piazza and reached tiny via Benedetto XIV, my ears caught strains of music on the air wafting from the inner space of the old city block to my left. The students from the nearby music conservatory were practicing. I changed my focus from the music still resonating in my consciousness to the concert floating around me.

Suddenly the peal of San Giacomo Maggiore's huge bells drowned out the students' practicing. Dong-dong-dong-dong. The sound reverberated in the stone streets and under the portico. As I turned left onto via San Vitale, the bell towers from Bologna's dozens of churches joined in the chorus. The music would serenade the city for 15 minutes: it was an evening ritual I had come to savor.

Their joyful pealing reminded me of the treasures I always found in Bologna: the hidden, seductive charm of her streets and her people. I unlocked the heavy, dark, wooden *portone* of the palazzo and went in. It slammed shut. The music of the ringing bells accompanied me up the stairs, another gift insinuating itself into my life.

www.ingramcontent.com/pod-product-compliance
Lightning Source LLC
Chambersburg PA
CBHW051850040426

42447CB00006B/778